DEVELOPMENT
Committee

Eugene R. Tempel

Book Four of the BoardSource Committee Series

uilding Effective Nonprofit Boards

erly the National Center for Nonprofit Boards

The Center on Philanthropy
at Indiana University
Indiana University–Purdue University Indianapolis

Library of Congress Cataloging-in-Publication Data

Tempel, Eugene R., 1947-
Development committee / by Eugene R. Tempel.
  p. cm. -- (Boardsource committee series ; bk. 4)
  ISBN 1-58686-072-0 pbk.
  1. Fund raising. 2. Nonprofit organizations--Finance.
  3. Boards of directors. I. Title. II. Series: Boardsource committee
  series ; 4
  HV41.2.T45 2004
  658.15'224--dc22
  2003021403

© 2004 BoardSource.
First printing, November 2003.
ISBN 1-58686-072-0

Published by BoardSource
1828 L Street, NW, Suite 900
Washington, DC 20036

BOARDSOURCE

Building Effective Nonprofit Boards

Formerly the National Center for Nonprofit Boards

BoardSource, formerly the National Center for Nonprofit Boards, is the premier resource for practical information, tools and best practices, training, and leadership development for board members of nonprofit organizations worldwide. Through our highly acclaimed programs and services, BoardSource enables organizations to fulfill their missions by helping build strong and effective nonprofit boards.

BoardSource provides assistance and resources to nonprofit leaders through workshops, training, and our extensive Web site, www.boardsource.org. A team of BoardSource governance consultants works directly with nonprofit leaders to design specialized solutions to meet organizations' needs and assists nongovernmental organizations around the world through partnerships and capacity building. As the world's largest, most comprehensive publisher of materials on nonprofit governance, BoardSource offers a wide selection of books, videotapes, and CDs. BoardSource also hosts the National Leadership Forum, bringing together approximately 800 governance experts, board members, and chief executives of nonprofit organizations from around the world.

Created out of the nonprofit sector's critical need for governance guidance and expertise, BoardSource is a 501c3 nonprofit organization that has provided practical solutions to nonprofit organizations of all sizes in diverse communities. In 2001, BoardSource changed its name from the National Center for Nonprofit Boards to better reflect its mission. Today, BoardSource has more than 15,000 members and has served more than 75,000 nonprofit leaders.

For more information, please visit our Web site at www.boardsource.org, e-mail us at mail@boardsource.org, or call us at 800-883-6262.

Have You Used These BoardSource Resources?

VIDEOS

Meeting the Challenge: An Orientation to Nonprofit Board Service

Speaking of Money: A Guide to Fund-Raising for Nonprofit Board Members

Building a Successful Team: A Guide to Nonprofit Board Development

BOOKS

The Board Chair Handbook

Managing Conflicts of Interest: Practical Guidelines for Nonprofit Boards

Checks and Balances: The Board Member's Guide to Nonprofit Financial Audits

The Board-Savvy CEO: How To Build a Strong, Positive Relationship with Your Board

Presenting: Board Orientation

Presenting: Nonprofit Financials

The Board Meeting Rescue Kit: 20 Ideas for Jumpstarting Your Board Meetings

The Board Building Cycle: Nine Steps to Finding, Recruiting, and Engaging Nonprofit Board Members

The Policy Sampler: A Resource for Nonprofit Boards

To Go Forward, Retreat! The Board Retreat Handbook

Nonprofit Board Answer Book: Practical Guide for Board Members and Chief Executives

Nonprofit Board Answer Book II: Beyond the Basics

The Legal Obligations of Nonprofit Boards

Self-Assessment for Nonprofit Governing Boards

Assessment of the Chief Executive

Fearless Fundraising

The Nonprofit Board's Guide to Bylaws

Creating and Using Investment Policies

Transforming Board Structure: New Possibilities for Committees and Task Forces

THE GOVERNANCE SERIES

1. Ten Basic Responsibilities of Nonprofit Boards

2. Financial Responsibilities of Nonprofit Boards

3. Structures and Practices of Nonprofit Boards

4. Fundraising Responsibilities of Nonprofit Boards

5. Legal Responsibilities of Nonprofit Boards

6. The Nonprofit Board's Role in Setting and Advancing the Mission

7. The Nonprofit Board's Role in Planning and Evaluation

8. How To Help Your Board Govern More and Manage Less

9. Leadership Roles in Nonprofit Governance

For an up-to-date list of publications and information about current prices, membership, and other services, please call BoardSource at 800-883-6262 or visit our Web site at www.boardsource.org.

Contents

Preface

The BoardSource Committee Series is intended to provide board members and chief executives with a practical approach to determining an appropriate committee structure and details on the responsibilities of each committee. The following preface will convey the philosophy of the series as a whole, using ideas from the first book in the series, Transforming Board Structure: Strategies for Committees and Task Forces, *and general information on how to handle committee operations.*

It is virtually impossible to define a committee structure that can or should be adopted by every nonprofit board. The material below can be used as a set of guidelines as your board searches for the best way to manage its own operations.

First and foremost, it is important to understand the difference between the full board, committees, and task forces in context of one another. The *board* has a fiduciary duty for the organization and is legally liable for its activities. It is responsible for articulating the direction for the organization and overseeing that the directives are implemented effectively and in an ethical manner. To manage these objectives, the board naturally must structure itself to accomplish its work in the most efficient manner possible.

Committees, or for the purpose of this introductory discussion, *standing committees*, are groups comprised of board members and outsiders that ensure consistency and regularity in key board practices. They are groups that are always necessary in helping the full board carry out its work. Committees with the executive committee as a common exception normally do not make organizational decisions; therefore, their members do not carry liability, as do members of the full board.

Task forces, similar in purpose to committees, are usually created in order to carry out a specific objective within a certain amount of time. They are typically established on an as-needed basis, allowing greater flexibility in the work of the board and its individual members. With the help of task forces, immediate needs of the board can be handled more quickly — without having to reconstruct the other committees and their ongoing work plans.

Committees and task forces generally do the majority of the board's work between meetings, allowing the full board to keep its attention on important decisions and on the big picture of the organization's success in fulfilling its mission. They give individual board members an opportunity to contribute to the work of the board in ways they would not be able to in regular meetings. These work groups enable the full board to benefit from the special skills and expertise of its members in a concrete manner.

How Committees Are Formed

To provide all the flexibility possible for your committee structure, avoid listing the job descriptions for your committees and task forces in the bylaws. A simple statement indicating that the board may form committees and other work groups as needed is sufficient. An exception to this approach, however, is the executive committee. If your board finds it necessary to form an executive committee, its authority must be detailed in your legal document. (Please refer to *Transforming Board Structure* or *Executive Committee* for more information.)

Your bylaws should also clarify who has the power to form committees. The full board should discuss and agree on the need for a specific committee or task force. Naturally, the board should also make the initial purpose of each standing committee or task force as explicit as possible to avoid any situations where the committee might establish its own charge or description of purpose. Responsibilities of each group may shift as circumstances change, so it is important to remain flexible in each group's charge. Usually the board chair chooses each committee chair and, in collaboration, they put together the rest of the group. Some boards require the chair's appointments to be approved by the board.

It is important to clarify the distinction between *board committees* and *organizational committees* in order to avoid any misunderstanding. Board committees report to the board and help carry out its mandate. Organizational committees, on the other hand, report to staff members and help with operational issues. They may serve as advisors to the staff and assist with issues that are staff members' responsibilities. In organizations with a small paid staff, organizational committees sometimes serve as volunteer staff to carry out the organization's work.

There is no reason for the board to duplicate staff work and form structures that collide with staff's duties. For example, if you have marketing staff, it is difficult to justify a board marketing committee. If your board includes marketing experts, there is nothing to prevent staff from asking for advice from knowledgeable board members — who should be happy to oblige. If there is no staff dedicated to organizational marketing efforts, your board may consider forming a task force to look at relevant issues affecting the organization in this area. It is also possible to form an organizational committee that is more operational and composed of staff members, board specialists, and probably outsider experts.

Job Descriptions, Membership, and Size

As mentioned above, each committee or task force should have a written charter explaining its role, responsibilities, and accountability. Although the full board is responsible for agreeing on the objectives for each work group, the committee chair is responsible for leading the group in following its charter and staying focused. The committee chair communicates with the board, ensuring that appropriate reporting takes place.

It is a good idea to include varying perspectives among committee members to ensure that all aspects of an issue or task receive adequate consideration. By rotating board members in and out of different committees, the board provides possibilities for individual development. It is probably not wise, however, for an individual board member to serve on more than two committees at a time because of possible burnout. Sometimes board members who have a particular interest in learning or contributing to a specific subject or cause will request or volunteer to be on a specific committee. Additionally, not all committees are comprised solely of board members. Community leaders who can share a particular area of expertise can add to the quality of discussion. Work groups are also a great way for someone who is interested in being a board member to begin involvement with an organization. Organizational committees typically draw members from the community who can add innovation and proficiency in a specific subject. There are few committees, however, that are usually comprised of only board members (e.g., the executive committee).

When deciding on the optimal committee size, once again, no specific rule exists. It strongly depends on the purpose of the committee, scope of the task, and the size of the full board. A committee should always be small enough to keep all members thoroughly involved. Group dynamics can determine effective working relationships and consequently influence the size of the group.

Committee-Staff Relationships

Some board committees or task forces benefit from direct staff support. The chief executive can assign a staff person to relevant committees to help with background information, relate the context of the committee work to operational work, or to provide administrative support. Work groups should be careful not to inundate the staff member with unreasonable requests; after all, he or she usually has other responsibilities in addition to committee support.

Meeting Schedule, Minutes, and Reports

Determining a meeting schedule for committees or task forces should be done on an as-needed basis — there is no particular prescription for the timing and minimum or maximum meetings per year. Each group knows what is expected and must be able to determine the necessary measures to accomplish the task. With committees that have members in various areas of the country or abroad, it is possible to communicate over the telephone or electronically, as long as the desired work is getting done properly. (State laws may regulate board meetings but not committee meetings.) One frequently *ineffective* way to manage most committee meetings, however, is to schedule them in conjunction with the full board meeting in an attempt to take advantage of all members gathering in the same place at the same time. This causes repetitious conversation and agenda items and, ultimately, may be waste of time.

Each group also has the freedom to determine how to keep track of what happens in committee meetings. Work groups may or may not find it necessary to keep minutes, but most likely want to take some notes for purposes of reporting to the board or to keep track of particularly detailed information. For example, a development committee drafting action plans for the coming fiscal year will need to document decisions carefully.

It is advisable to circulate committee reports as part of the board consent agenda in the board package. This allows board members to familiarize themselves with the contents before the meeting and helps to eliminate the tradition of spending meeting time listening to committee reports. Major issues needing board debate should be placed on the main agenda.

Assessing the Need for Committees or Task Forces

In coming up with the most advantageous committee structure for your board, make sure that you continuously reassess the need for each work group. Unnecessary committees simply waste people's valuable time, misuse members' contributions and commitment, and provide no added value to the board. Some boards rely on a *zero-based committee structure*, disbanding all non-standing committees and task forces at the end of the year and reevaluating their necessity for the future — they start with a clean slate. It may still happen that a committee of the previous year gets reinstated but it may have a new composition of members or it may have a slightly changed charter. Whatever method your board uses to justify its internal structure, make sure that, ultimately, you have only committees and task forces that your organization needs and that they have all the resources necessary to function efficiently.

INTRODUCING THE SERIES

As we discussed above, there is no single right answer on how to structure a board or indicate how committees or task forces meet their expectations. Structures should never remain static and all boards should keep an open mind when experimenting with different options. Constant evaluation and flexibility are necessary during the search for optimal results. The best way to keep a committee structure simple is to limit the number of standing committees to what is absolutely essential, and to supplement these committees with less permanent structures.

With the Committee Series, BoardSource is providing additional information and guidance to help your board determine its structural options. The initial series consists of six books. The first book, *Transforming Board Structure*, sets the stage for committees in general. The next five books each cover the duties of common committees that many boards find necessary.

- *Transforming Board Structure* — introducing committee and task force structure

- *Governance Committee* Book One — relating to recruitment and education of board members

- *Executive Committee* (Book Two) — addressing how to use executive committees properly

- *Financial Committees* (Book Three) — defining the core duties of the finance, audit, and investment committees

- *Development Committee* Book Four — helping to involve your full board in fundraising

- *Advisory Councils* Book Five — describing the numerous roles that advisory groups or councils can play to help your nonprofit function more efficiently

Acknowledgments

Some of the concepts presented here were taken or adapted from research at the Center on Philanthropy at Indiana University; much of the material was developed at The Fund Raising School at the Center on Philanthropy. I thank my colleagues on the faculty and staff of The Fund Raising School and at the Center on Philanthropy for the material to support this book.

Introduction

"What you have to do and the way you have to do it is incredibly simple. Whether you are willing to do it, that's another matter."

— Peter Drucker

And so it is with board involvement in fundraising…

Responsibility for the nonprofit sector in the United States rests firmly in the hands of millions of volunteers who serve as board members for nonprofit organizations. Although board members have broad legal requirements and basic reporting duties, they ultimately are largely self-regulated. Nonprofit organizations that are successful over time usually owe their vitality in large measure to the work of committed and thoughtful board members. In Fisher Howe's *Welcome to the Board*, he outlines seven responsibilities that each board member must not overlook in order to ensure the success of an organization — fundraising is one of them.[1] Ensuring adequate resources are available for the organization to function effectively is one of the key aspects of nonprofit board governance. Because this is such an essential aspect of board member stewardship — individually and as a whole — it is important to have a group of people involved who can lead the efforts in fundraising.

It is easier to declare, however, that the entire board should be involved in fundraising than it is to enlist each individual board member's support and move the program forward. Creating a development committee helps ensure that coordination and oversight of the board's fundraising

---

1. Howe, Fisher. *Welcome to the Board: Your Guide to Effective Participation.* San Francisco: Jossey-Bass, 1995.

process is under control. It is essential to remember that while a development committee centers everyone's attention on this essential task, ultimate responsibility for the financial state of the organization, including fundraising, lies with the *entire* board.

Fundraising must begin with the board, because board members hold the level of understanding and commitment necessary to fulfill the organization's mission. They are current donors who have made thoughtful commitments or should be challenged to do so to sustain the work of the organization. The board's oversight gives it the knowledge, integrity, and credibility in making the case for support to peers, corporate and foundation leaders, and others who might care about the cause. As primary advocates and vested donors who are committed to the organization, board members are in the best position to ask others to make gifts and to secure volunteers to seek gifts from others. When members of the board participate it sends a clear signal of the organization's commitment to the fulfillment of the mission. Thus, fundraising begins with the board.

The degree of board involvement in fundraising and the need to have a board committee focused on that task are viewpoints not shared by all board experts. John Carver, for example, argues that boards should be focused primarily on governing an organization, thereby ensuring sound performance. Responsibilities such as fundraising are viewed as secondary functions and should only be undertaken when the board sees it as essential for organizational effectiveness. More important than raising funds, he would contend, would be proper governance to form an organization "worth raising funds for."[2]

Agreed, governance is the primary task of board members. We will explore in this book the idea that good governance includes securing the future of the organization largely through maintaining accountability to constituents, which forms the basis of successful fundraising. Board members must raise funds to keep the organization financially solvent. They must inform the public of the organization's worthiness for philanthropic support. They must hold the organization accountable for public use of its resources.

This book is designed to help your organization evaluate its need for a development committee, how to structure it — either as a board committee or an organizational committee — and how to guide its work. The book outlines responsibilities of the committee in general, of board members in particular, and the roles of the staff in working together with the board in order to find success in fundraising.

---

2. Carver, John. *On Board Leadership*. San Francisco: Jossey-Bass, 2002.

1 ROLES AND RESPONSIBILITIES OF DEVELOPMENT COMMITTEES

By creating a development committee as part of your board, you are establishing a deeper level of focus and creativity in plans for fundraising and soliciting gifts. Because fundraising is such an important role of governing boards, it is certainly advantageous, if not necessary, to structure a development committee to stay focused on fundraising and engage a work group of this type.

The development committee typically works with the board chair, the chief executive, the chief development officer CDO, and other development staff to provide valuable input for developing the fundraising plan and engaging the entire board in fundraising. The committee's responsibilities may include but are not limited to the following:

- Involving and motivating other board members and volunteers in cultivation and solicitation of gifts

- Helping to develop policies for board and staff action related to gift solicitation and recognition

- Ensuring that the case for support is strong, current, and based on the organization's mission and goals

- Helping to develop strategies for involvement and cultivation of major gift prospects

- Providing information on environmental factors affecting fundraising among the organization's constituencies

- Helping to evaluate potential prospects for increased contributions

- Helping to develop expectations for financial contributions from the board, and providing leadership by making their own gifts

- Soliciting gifts at levels required for annual, special, and planned giving programs

- Participating actively in special events and providing leadership for capital campaigns

- Developing and signing solicitation and acknowledgment letters

It is not possible to create a task list that applies to all development committees or the same board during all of its life cycles. The list will need to be altered as the organization grows or develops other revenue sources. Whether there is staff to help coordinate the efforts or whether outside volunteers are engaged in detailed work has an impact on what the committee needs to accomplish. Dividing these responsibilities among other board committees or the entire board can cause neglect of important fundraising tasks, especially those not directly related to solicitation. A development committee can work with development staff to ensure that the organization's fundraising is based on good information and planning, receives the attention it deserves, and reaches its full potential.

But on a large board or on a board where much is done by standing committees, the development committee can help engage the board in fundraising without detracting from its oversight responsibilities. On a smaller board, the development committee can be a good way to engage other volunteers to advance the mission of the organization and its fundraising process. Each board must assess its need for a separate development committee and clarify its role and relationship with the rest of the board members.

BOARD MEMBERS IN ACTION

Board members often find tension between fulfilling their policy roles and serving as good stewards without becoming deeply involved in operations. The board's fundraising work requires "role inversion" — taking a hands-on approach in the act of fundraising for the organization, rather than solely providing leadership and strategy. Board members, whose chief role is usually oversight and setting policy, are asked to invert that role when they take on "staff-type" functions as they become engaged in fundraising. They must take direction from the development staff and depend on them for guidance and support. On occasion, they must be willing to set aside their policy-making roles and work directly with staff in carrying out their fundraising tasks. The staff and the board orientation process must help development committee and board members understand their distinctly different roles as policy makers and fundraisers.

Sometimes the existence of a development committee causes an expectation among board members that the development committee will take care of all the board's fundraising work. The fundraising staff and the development committee must educate the full board and guard against this expectation. The entire board must not only retain the responsibility for fundraising; it must also engage in fundraising tasks as the members' talents and experience allow. There are a number of ways discussed later in this book for all board members to be involved in fundraising.

2 BUILDING THE DEVELOPMENT COMMITTEE

INTERNAL STRUCTURE

Traditionally, we look at development committees as board committees whose role is to engage the entire board in fundraising. Other structural options for development committees, however, do exist. Defining what the organization needs to achieve in terms of fundraising, assessing the quality of resources it already has put in place, and analyzing the capacity of the board and staff to reach these goals help organizations develop appropriate structures.

The traditional development committee of the board is a key group in the development process. Its members are active in planning for and conducting fundraising. The group works closely with development staff and the chair of the committee boosts the participation of the rest of the board. This particular structure for a development committee is still the most common in fundraising nonprofits.

Some boards, however, simply decide to act as a fundraising committee of the whole. The entire board shares the duties and carries the load. Eliminating a separate development committee of the board is sometimes a deliberate effort to stress the duty for each board member to participate in fundraising, and not simply leave it to the development committee members.

An *organizational* development committee works directly with the development staff and may be composed of staff members, community leaders, fundraising specialists, helpful volunteers who want to be involved and who have special skills, and board members who have particular expertise and aptitude in representing the organization to their funders. The size of the committee may be quite substantial, to ensure greater reach, but cannot exceed the staff available to oversee and support the committee's activities.

The size of any type of development committee will depend on the enormity and variety of the activities, the complexity of the fundraising approaches, and the size of the board and volunteer resources available. Naturally, an organizational committee tends to be much larger than a board committee, as there the tasks usually are multifaceted and more hands-on. A larger size allows for a better distribution of duties and inclusion of various skills.

Subcommittees and Task Forces

Organizations with more developed fundraising programs may want to use subcommittees and/or task forces to help with specialized fundraising activities. Volunteers from outside the board can also serve on these subcommittees or task forces. If the subcommittee reports to the development committee, it should be chaired by a member of the development committee. Most of the members, however, could be other volunteers. Typical subcommittees include the following:

- **Special Events Committee:** This subcommittee might accept responsibility for organizing ongoing special events. One-time special events may be organized by a temporary task force.

- **Annual Fund Committee:** If there is no staff, this subcommittee typically plans and implements the organization's annual fund. Often it subdivides its activity by gift level or donor market such as individual, corporate, foundation, and others.

- **Corporate and Foundation Committee:** The unique approach required for corporate and foundation gifts sometimes calls for the development of a special subcommittee to focus on major grants from these sources. Members are usually selected because of linkages to corporations and foundations, and special staff related to corporate and foundation proposal development.

- **Major Gifts Committee:** This subcommittee helps to identify potential major gifts, donors, and strategies for cultivation, as well as develops strategies to involve donors in partnership with the organization, resulting in major gifts. This group will host events, help develop proposals, and participate in individual, face-to-face solicitation.

- **Planned Giving Committee:** Organizations with endowments, supporters who remember the particular organization in their wills, and/or deferred giving mechanisms need extensive staff support to manage the program, with board members' input remaining invaluable. This subcommittee includes board members familiar with planned giving instruments and capacity to identify planned giving prospects as well as key development staff. Board members help develop organizational policies for planned gifts, host seminars on planned giving, and provide their expertise to staff in the planned giving process.

- **Capital Campaign Task Force:** When an organization undertakes a capital campaign, board commitment is essential. The chair of the board would lead this task force in engaging the key leaders in the initial planning. After the campaign chair has been elected, he or she will most likely take on the responsibility to ensure that numerous separate committees and task forces are formed in order to accomplish the vast array of activities that compose a successful capital campaign.

Each development committee naturally determines its own composition and internal elements. There is no need to add new subcommittees if the committee's list of duties is limited and the scope of activities straightforward. The more complicated the tasks assigned to the committee, the easier it is to accomplish them if special skills and expertise are brought together in smaller task forces or subcommittees.

COMMITTEE MEMBERSHIP AND RECRUITMENT

The board's development committee should always be chaired by a member of the board who has the contacts, knowledge, enthusiasm, and skills to lead the board's fundraising effort, as well as the ability to involve other board members in the process. The chair of the development committee is responsible for setting an example in making gifts and taking on fundraising tasks both for the development committee and for the entire board. If the organization has specialized fundraising staff such as special events, annual fund, or major gifts staff, they should coordinate their efforts appropriately with the board committee. (Please see Chapter 3 for a more in-depth discussion of responsibilities and communication between board/committee members and staff.)

Especially if there is no organizational development committee, the development committee of the board should include nonmembers of the board. In fact, it makes sense that fundraising committees involve community volunteers in addition to board members. Often, volunteers with outside connections to the community can increase the committee's potential for success. They add valuable time on tasks and extend the "workforce" available to the fundraising process. Most types of development committees offer excellent opportunities to involve non-board member volunteers and are a good way to prospect for future board members. However, the committee should include a core of at least three to six board members who can ensure further that the work of the committee is grounded in the organization's mission.

Recruiting volunteers to the development committee can be a challenging task. Today, many retired volunteers prefer to use their professional skills in the volunteer work they become involved in. A retired accountant may be more interested in volunteering to do finance work; a former public relations manager may prefer to find marketing opportunities. Many younger volunteers are interested in ad hoc activities, often preferring to volunteer with their friends and in direct service to clients. For these reasons, recruitment for the development committee should also focus on those already engaged in other activities at the organization, who may have developed a passion for the organization's mission.

It is imperative for development committee members to be knowledgeable about the organization's community and its constituencies, especially major gift prospects. In general, individuals who have good people skills are perfect candidates for the committee. The following list highlights specific skills to look for in development committee members:

- Individuals who have engaging personalities, who are articulate, and who are not afraid to seek out prospects

- People who are comfortable discussing finances with others

- People with access to individual, corporate, or foundation resources

- Those who hold successful experience with and commitment to aspects of volunteer fundraising

- Individuals who radiate confidence and trust as the representatives of the organization

There are other helpful skills and expertise for development committee members, especially those in an organization without development staff. These skills include writing and presentation skills, successful experience raising money, interpersonal and listening skills, financial and strategic planning expertise, knowledge of tax law, fundraising management, computer systems and databases, and the ability to involve and train other members of the board. When there is development staff to coordinate the overall fundraising plan, committee members translate the general guidelines for the rest of the board and oversee that each board member follows the unified front and respects the detailed guidance of the plan.

Development committee members must join with other volunteers and staff in a dedicated team effort. This group should constantly evaluate its composition and work with the board to identify nominees with the diversity, skills, and backgrounds they need. A grid that lists committee members and the qualifications and specific skills needed may be helpful. (See Appendix III for a committee member checklist.)

TRAINING FOR COMMITTEE MEMBERS

Members of the development committee should be trained in every aspect of their work and receive an orientation to fundraising. Besides the actual skills in fundraising methods and cultivation of potential donors, committee members may benefit from guidance on how to involve peers and how to get them excited about the activities that the development team needs to accomplish. Staff may provide an introduction to the resources that the organization can provide for board members and explain how board members will be able to take advantage of the database and other technical means available to them.

Some board members or fundraising volunteers, however, can either in their enthusiasm or lack of training cross socially responsible lines. These "mavericks" can do damage to an organization's fundraising program. They might negotiate gifts that do not fit the organization's mission, or they may inadvertently "overpromise" what the organization might be able to do in meeting donor expectations. The more training board members and other fundraising volunteers have, the more potential there is to mitigate these situations.

3 THE RELATIONSHIPS BETWEEN COMMITTEE MEMBERS AND STAFF

WHY BOARD-STAFF COMMUNICATION IS IMPORTANT IN FUNDRAISING

Simply having the right people on the development committee does not ensure success. Board members and other volunteers generally carry out their fundraising activities with the initiative of development *staff* coordinating with the development committee. The idea of this initiative coming from the staff is not out of the ordinary.

Organizations with professional development staff sometimes have staff members directly involved in both asking for gifts themselves and in supporting and accompanying board members in the fundraising process. Staff members should be aware of their responsibility for anticipating fundraising needs, assigning tasks, and knowing how to give "gentle" reminders to the board; committee and board members should also be aware of their own responsibility to carry tasks they accept and to stay in touch with staff throughout the fundraising process. In this practice, staff communicates its day-to-day knowledge of the organization and its needs to the board — supporting volunteers and committee and board members to use their skills, contacts, and passion for the mission. Sometimes committee and board members want to be told what to do or to be asked to carry out very specific tasks by the development staff. This provides them with a starting place and supplies them with the motivation they need.

Board members and volunteers generally prefer a relationship of interdependence with staff members. They do not want to feel controlled by staff, but they do want guidance and direction, as discussed above. Members and volunteers need staff members who share the necessary support and help them meet their obligations in order to fulfill the organization's expectations. Board members and other volunteers want to succeed in the fundraising tasks they undertake; therefore, constant communication and role sharing between board and staff is essential. Development staff must keep the volunteers and board members focused on the specific actions required for successful fundraising. Board and committee members must ask direct questions of the development staff in order to feel fully educated in relaying the needs of the organization to the public.

THE DEVELOPMENT COMMITTEE AND STAFF

The development committee of the board usually works closest with the chief executive in a small organization where no fundraising staff exists. In a larger organization, however, the chief development officer CDO guides and provides direction to the development committee. This is nearly always the case when there is an organizational development committee. The chief development officer works closely with the chair of the development committee. He or she provides information, develops materials, calls meetings, and schedules appointments with the committee. The CDO also provides committee members with materials and reminds them of appointments and follow-up contacts. If the fundraising staff includes specialized personnel for such functions as special events, the annual fund, major gifts, and planned gifts, those staff members should engage board members and other volunteers to those efforts. Figure 1 provides a more comprehensive look at the roles of board members and staff.

FIGURE 1:
FUNDRAISING ROLES AMONG BOARD AND STAFF

Staff	Board
Provides information about the organization	Learns the mission and goals of the organization
Develops proposals and letters	Provides information about prospects
Provides first drafts and coordinates the mailing of solicitation letters	Provides final edits of and signs personalized solicitation letters
Schedules solicitation rehearsals and meetings	Practices solicitation calls with team members
Provides follow up to all solicitation calls	Uses linkages to set appointments
Sends reminders and organizes reports of meetings	Solicits gifts on behalf of the organization
Provides information about programs and tax advantages in a solicitation call	Asks for the gift in a solicitation meeting
Sends acknowledgments of donations	Sends a personal note of thanks

Remember, fundraising is the chief responsibility that requires board members to stray from their normal oversight and policy-setting role to engage in fundraising and work more closely with staff. This can be a difficult transition to make, but it is one that is absolutely necessary in ensuring credibility and strength in an organization's fundraising methods.

Communication Risks between Board and Staff

Tension can arise in the relationships among the chief executive, the CDO, and others in various fundraising leadership positions when board members are engaged in fundraising. Because members of the development staff build strong relationships with members of the development committee and other members on the board, a high level of trust between the chief executive and the development staff is essential.

The CDO and other development staff members have a responsibility not to use relationships with board members for purposes other than fundraising. Doing so can erode the relationships between the chief executive and the board and can lead to organizational distrust. Development staff members who use relationships with board members to advance their own agenda or to lobby for priorities different from those being promoted by the chief executive undermine the integrity of the organization. Committee members should be wary of staff who go beyond the fundraising relationship in their support of the committee's work and seek counsel or audience on other organizational matters.

Working Together

To ensure a good working relationship, guiding both board members and staff in working together is key in successful team building. Board members should be introduced to the strengths of staff members and the support they can provide, including fundraising expertise, knowledge of the community and the organization's donors and prospective donors, and understanding the details of the organization's programs. Equally as important, staff members benefit from training that focuses on how to lead fundraising by example, without controlling and micromanaging board members. Staff should also be reminded of the peer relationships board members have with donors and prospective donors as well as the credibility they bring to the process. With intentional training, tensions that can occur between board members and staff over fundraising assignments and activities can be kept to a minimum as each group understands the other's role and they learn to see each other as partners on a team rather than individuals with separate tasks.

4 DEVELOPING THE FUNDRAISING PLAN

No development effort is effective without a comprehensive plan. This is true for small organizations as well as major nonprofits with budgets of millions of dollars. The development committee is in a key position to help with planning as the board's role in general is to steer the organization in the right direction with sufficient resources.

A development plan ensures that your organization meets its financial goals. It must take a comprehensive look at what needs to be accomplished so that the work of the organization is completed successfully. The plan must analyze and choose the appropriate strategies to meet these goals. What are potentially the most productive methods of bringing in revenue? What is a cost-effective approach to reach the donors? Who are the donors? The plan must outline the time frame for the various development activities and assign responsibilities for the players in the plan. It must ensure that the needed statements, documents, and brochures are ready. It must assess the priorities among the various programs and determine how the operational budget will be covered through effective fundraising methods. A development plan must also realize that raising funds costs money — fundraising expenses must be included in the master budget.

A fundraising plan is an essential part of any organization's strategic or long-range plan. The development committee can help provide a comprehensive look at the resources currently being raised by the organization, what realistically can and should be raised in the future, and provide benchmarks that can measure organizational success in fundraising.

The committee is also responsible for the resources and training needed to involve each board member and volunteer. Involving the development committee in these aspects of planning for fundraising ensures a good fundraising plan and a viable organizational mission. It also helps create success in fundraising by creating ownership among the organization's front-line volunteer fundraisers.

PLANNING AND FUNDRAISING RESPONSIBILITIES

One cause of discord in many nonprofits is the confusion over fundraising roles. Each organization must determine who is actually responsible for bringing in grants and donations, and who determines the overall strategy and policies. It is important to delineate which tasks belong to the staff and what duties are carried out by the board and the committee before the raising of funds actually begins. Without a true understanding of fundraising as part of the overall financial plan and without appropriate division of labor, it is difficult to secure a strong fiscal base for the organization. The board and the chief executive need to be on the same page in this issue before planning stages move on to action.

FUNDRAISING METHODS

Nonprofit organizations have many options for generating income. In addition to fees or revenue from products and services, and contracts with and grants from government or other agencies, they can raise philanthropic support through other methods of fundraising. These options for fundraising include:

- writing proposals to foundations
- solicitation of funds through direct mail
- reliance on annual campaigns and phone-a-thons
- major events underwritten by corporate sponsorships
- small-scale special events as part of the annual calendar
- major gift solicitation
- capital campaigns
- planned giving
- board members' personal contributions

Organizations should set a good method of implementing a total development program that includes all of the approaches in the box above. The organization should make an appropriate choice for fundraising based on its scope and donor base and incorporate the activities in the overall fundraising plan. The board itself is responsible for drafting the necessary policies related to appropriate gift acceptance and ensuring that these guidelines are compatible with the mission of the organization.

In larger organizations with greater potential, the chief executive might spend a significant part of his or her time on cultivation of major funders. Development staff allows for growth and diversification of all fundraising efforts. The development director is usually the coordinator of the overall plan. He or she finds the best way to take advantage of the chief executive's time, to collaborate with the board in order to utilize the contacts that board members bring with them, and to hire and supervise the rest of the development staff.

THE PLAN ITSELF

Getting Started

Staff members with access to organizational data and information are in the best position to prepare the draft of the development plan. (Development committee members can provide information from the external environment where funds will be sought to help tie the fundraising plan to the organization's overall strategic plan, as we have discussed previously.)

The development committee can also give input to the goals for each subunit of the total fundraising effort. Chairs of the special task forces can act as helpful resources on respective detailed operational data on the groups. The amount to be raised through special events, direct mail, new gifts, repeated gifts, upgraded gifts, major gifts, capital gifts, and planned gifts all add up to the total fundraising income that the organization hopes to achieve. These goals should be fully integrated into the overall fundraising plan. Finally, the committee can work with staff to determine strategies for accomplishing goals and assigning board member responsibilities.

An organization's fundraising plan must have a diversification of sources: It is not wise to rely solely on a few major gifts. When creating the overall plan, it is important to ask the following questions:

- What sources of philanthropic support are available to us?

- Where can board involvement be best leveraged to meet fundraising goals?

- What training and resources will board members need in order to feel prepared?

- What does our organization need to do to cultivate new donors in order to be positioned where we want to be in the next few years?

Planning Sequence

After board and staff work together to find the best answers to these questions and formulate a plan that is right for their organization, a planning sequence must be implemented. The following steps provide a suggested planning sequence for fundraising:

1. **Merge planning**

   - Align the fundraising plan with the overall strategic plan and the financial goals of the organization.

   - Achieve an integrated approach to organizational planning.

2. **Define organization**

   - Review the organization's mission, goals, and objectives from the perspective of its donor constituencies.

   - Achieve a donor-friendly organization.

3. **Develop and refine the case for support**

   - Write a compelling case statement that provides the rationale for your fundraising efforts.

   - Achieve a consolidated representation of the organization and its efforts.

4. **Gather facts**

   - Collect preliminary needs, gift history, donor history, prospect base, volunteer base, fundraising vehicles, market studies, public relations resources, and technical and production support.

   - Achieve a fundraising approach that is based on facts and not on assumptions.

5. **Determine and validate needs**

   - Establish program and operational needs, special purpose needs, minor and major capital needs, and endowment needs, and confirm that each need can and should be met.

   - Achieve results that meet the actual needs of the organization.

6. **Consider vehicles**

   - Reflect on annual funds, special gifts, capital campaigns, and planned giving.

   - Achieve fundraising goals by using the right tools appropriate for the scope of your efforts.

7. **Consider markets**

   - Be sure to include individuals, associations, congregations, corporations, commerce, foundations, and government.

   - Achieve fundraising goals by approaching appropriate donor "markets."

8. **List and evaluate resources**

   - Assess staff, space, equipment, promotional material, budget, and volunteers available.

   - Achieve cost effectiveness by working within your means.

9. **Determine fundraising goals**

   - Decide the level of philanthropic support to be sought over a set period of time.

   - Achieve all the goals because they were reasonable.

10. **Prepare a plan**

    - Determine timetables and sequences for initiating communications, involvement, leadership development, and solicitation.

    - Achieve timely results and meet your deadlines.

11. **Install and use control mechanisms**

    - Determine overall structure, outline reporting structures, and assign responsibilities.

    - Achieve accountability through project ownership.

By outlining the sequential steps for your planning, you will attempt to complete each move before turning to the next task. If you include desired outcomes with each step, you will remain motivated to look ahead until the entire process is finished.

Key Areas of Planning for the Committee To Address

The development committee can provide unique insight into the resource issues that the organization must confront in its planning process. Committee feedback starts the coordination process by aligning all financial efforts within the strategic framework to meet the organizational objectives. Fundraising is not a separate activity by itself. It is an important part of securing an overall sound financial base.

Case for Support and Communication Tools

The case for support defines all the possible reasons why a donor should support a particular organization or one of its projects. The case for support is based on the organization's mission and its plan for the future. It does not focus on internal organizational needs, but it focuses on the external, societal needs to be fulfilled; diminishing the suffering of individuals, increasing the beauty and pleasures in life, or affecting change in any positive manner. External expressions of the case can take many forms, including brochures and newsletters, as well as the information presented in face-to-face conversations with donors and prospective donors. Figure 2 provides more specific information to present in favor of your organization for each case component. Appendix IV gives more information on using the case for support in a communications toolkit for board members.

FIGURE 2
COMPONENTS OF THE CASE FOR SUPPORT

Case Components	Must Articulate
Mission	Awareness, Insight to Problem
Goals	Desired Achievement
Objectives	What's in Place
Programs	Service to People Stories
Governing Board	Character, Quality of Organization
Staffing	Qualifications, Strengths
Facilities and Equipment	Advantages, Strengths, Effectiveness
Finances	Validate Need for Philanthropy
Planning and Evaluation	Documents, Commitments, Strengths, Impact
History	Heroic Saga, Credibility

Source: Indiana University Center on Philanthropy © The Fund Raising School.

Determining Fundraising Goals and Methods

Organizations often determine fundraising goals based on projected deficits. While this is very tempting as a simple, straightforward approach, it can be a formula for failure. Generally, internal financial needs are only one factor in the amount of funds that can be raised. Responsible planning starts with realistic expectations. The overall financial plan should address unexpected (or sometimes temporarily calculated) deficits. Fundraising's purpose should not be to correct financial miscalculations and short falls. Fundraising is a means to advance the mission over the long run.

The development committee and the development staff can use their expertise to determine fundraising methods and goals based on the following factors:

- Strength of the case for support (including the financial resources required to fulfill the mission)

- History of fundraising success

- Potential for upgraded gifts

- Potential for acquiring new donors

- Staff and volunteer resources available

- Financial resources available

- Knowledge of the external environment

- Economic conditions

- Other fundraising efforts that might be used for approaching the organization's donors

By concentrating on the most appropriate methods and defining the most reasonable and reachable goals for fundraising, the development committee and staff can manage to eliminate activities that are less effective or inappropriate for the scope or mission of the organization. Unattainable goals temper motivation and momentum. This does not mean goals should be set at easily attainable levels. Rather, goals should be reasonably set with some incentive to exceed the expectations.

5 HOW THE COMMITTEE WORKS TO MOTIVATE AND INVOLVE THE REST OF THE BOARD

Ideally, *all* board members should be involved in fundraising. At a minimum, the development committee and the entire board must strive for 100 percent participation in annual giving. Every board member should be a donor in order to express his or her commitment to the organization's mission. Board members who give significant time and gifts-in-kind should still be encouraged to contribute financially. Gifts of time and gifts-in-kind generally do not convince a potential donor of the board member's commitment to the organization. Board members who have not made significant, proportional gifts will find it challenging to solicit gifts from others outside the organization.

DETERMINING HOW TO BEST INVOLVE EACH BOARD MEMBER

First and foremost, it is important to realize that **board members need to be involved in fundraising *individually*, based on their skills and abilities**. The process of determining board member optimal involvement can be time-consuming but is worth the investment. If this has not been done before, members of the development committee should contact other members of the board individually to assess each person's strengths, skill level, and overall readiness for fundraising. Then members of the committee can determine which tasks should be assigned and to whom.

During this assessment period, the committee members must evaluate individual board members' strengths and readiness to raise funds. Committee members must match each person's level of capability to particular needs of the organization in order to determine how each board member can play a special role. Initially, some board members may not feel comfortable making personal calls to solicit gifts. As an introduction to fundraising involvement, members should be assigned tasks matched to their abilities and comfort levels. Some might participate in planning special events; others might write letters thanking donors or soliciting small gifts. The committee needs to work directly with staff to assign achievable duties to board members, at which they can succeed. The list on page 19 highlights possible areas of involvement for committee members, board members, staff, and volunteers.

AREAS OF INVOLVEMENT

The following list highlights many ways for board members to be involved in the fundraising process (in order of direct involvement):

- Make a personal contribution.

- Write thank you notes for gift acknowledgment.

- Participate in strategic and development planning.

- Provide prospective donor information.

- Add names to mailing lists.

- Write personal notes on solicitation letters.

- Introduce potential donors to members of the organization.

- Write a support letter to a government agency, foundation, or corporation.

- Seek out donations for a special event or help plan a special event.

- Cultivate relationships with potential donors.

- Make a solicitation call with other volunteers and/or board members.

As you can see, there are many ways to involve both experienced and inexperienced committee members in addition to personal solicitations.

Major Gifts

Usually, the best way for board members to leverage their individual roles within the organization is to be involved in the identification, cultivation, and solicitation of major gift donors. In a total development plan, asking for any size gift is only one step in the overall process. Smaller gifts lead to larger gifts. Smaller gifts might be raised through the mail. Major gifts, however, are raised through personal solicitation made by key staff and board members. There is a saying that successful major gifts are as simple as having the *right* volunteer solicit the *right* prospect for the *right* amount for the *right* cause at the *right* time. Often these "right" volunteers are members of the development committee or board members who have a connection to the potential donor. Figure 3 will be helpful in understanding the different choices and levels of effectiveness in soliciting gifts from outsiders. As you can see, personal asks are the most effective means of securing a gift.

FIGURE 3
HIERARCHY OF EFFECTIVENESS IN GIFT SOLICITATION

MOST EFFECTIVE

Personal: face-to-face

Personal letter on personal stationery
or personal telephone calls

Personalized letter/Internet

Phonation/Telephone solicitation

Impersonal telephone/Telemarketing

Direct mail/Impersonal letter/Internet

Special event/Fundraising benefit

Door-to-door

Media advertising

LEAST EFFECTIVE

Source: Indiana University Center on Philanthropy © The Fund Raising School.

All members of the development committee and the board should be encouraged to move from less personal to more personal solicitation. The development staff should work in concert with the development committee to move the committee and board members up this hierarchy of effectiveness in solicitation of gifts. Less experienced board members may be used in the less effective areas as a means of training and initial foundation for building a deeper level of comfort in fundraising tasks.

Steps in the Major Gifts Process

Successful major gift solicitation is a process that may take years. Development committee members work with development staff to identify potential donors and categorize them in diverse gift classes. Different donors may be receptive to different methods of cultivation. Gifts may come in numerous forms: from a one-time check to installment payments; from bequests to deferred-giving vehicles.

Cultivation of potential donors and stewardship of major gifts means continuous communication. This is why personal contacts and direct interaction are so important. Board members can contribute greatly to this process. Please see page 22 for a list of responsibilities and areas of contribution from board and committee members.

Board Involvement in Identifying Potential Donors

Nonprofit organizations are constantly searching for new donors and for current donors who are prospects for larger gifts. Ultimately, the process leads to the five "rights" that must coincide for major gift success (discussed on page 19). Members of the development committee assist with the organizational process of identifying and engaging these prospective donors and involve the full board in the process. The organization may use special events, direct mail, and other means for identifying new donor prospects. Development committee members can provide the names of individuals and entities that should be added to mailing lists as potential new donors based on *linkage, ability,* and *interest.* In this process, linkage suggests a connection between the prospective donor and an individual associated with the nonprofit organization; ability means the prospective donor has the means to make a gift at the level being asked; interest means the prospective donor is interested in the mission, goals, and objectives of the organization and has values that make the case for support

Initial linkages begin with the development committee. The committee also should organize the full board to provide the names of prospective donors based on linkage, ability, and interest. Various volunteers may also provide important linkages to prospective donors. The organization can provide the development committee with prospect identification forms and set goals for new prospect identification monthly, quarterly, or at each committee meeting.

The Development Committee's Responsibilities to Major Gifts

1. **Identification:** Members assist in identifying potential major gift donors based on their own personal knowledge of linkage, ability, and interest.

2. **Qualification:** Members assist the organization in determining how likely a prospective donor might be to make a major gift and at what level.

3. **Development of Strategy:** Members help determine specific strategies for potential major donors based on their knowledge of the prospective donor level of engagement and interests.

4. **Cultivation:** Members assist in efforts to involve prospective donors more closely with the organization, inform them of potential projects, and determine approaches for solicitation.

5. **Solicitation and Negotiation:** Members join soliciting teams to make personal calls with other volunteers or organizational representatives to ask for major gifts and negotiate for gift amounts and terms.

6. **Acknowledgment:** Members express gratitude directly to those donors whom they have solicited and make certain that the organization has processes for acknowledging all gifts.

7. **Stewardship:** Members make certain that major gifts are used for intended purposes and report to major donors on the impact of their gift.

8. **Renewal:** Members help determine when it might be appropriate to approach a major donor for another major gift and essentially begin the eight-step process again.

Source: Adapted from the Center on Philanthropy at Indiana University © The Fund Raising School.

The development committee identifies prospects from among the organization's existing donor base and engages other board members in this prospect development process. Every donor is a prospective donor for a gift at a higher level. By evaluating the strength of the donor's interest in the organization, the donor's level of engagement with the organization, the level of resources that the donor has available, and the appropriate linkages with the organization, members of the development committee can assist in developing strategies for building partnerships with donors that lead to larger gifts. For a specific example of identification and evaluation for potential prospects, please see Silent Prospecting on page 24.

Other methods of identifying prospective donors include noting expressed interests of colleagues, paying attention to noteworthy financial events, tracking achievements, and hosting involvement activities.

Personal Solicitation of Major Gifts

Board members and volunteers involved in soliciting gifts become advocates and askers on behalf of the organization based on its mission and case for support. Donors respond to the organization and to the board members or volunteers. As illustrated below, there is always some part of the asker in every aspect of solicitation. However, if the solicitation is based on the case for support, this part can be minimized.

ASPECTS OF SOCIAL EXCHANGE

1. Advocate/asker internalizes value and values of organization.

2. Advocate/asker becomes exemplar of organization and extension of its value and values.

3. Advocate/asker and organization understand that:

   • Every gift contains a bit of the donor's "self."

   • A sensitive and appropriate acknowledgment is required.

4. Asking and giving involves all (organization, asker, donor) in a shared enterprise.

Source: Adapted from the Center on Philanthropy at Indiana University © The Fund Raising School.

SILENT PROSPECTING

"Silent prospecting" is one way in which the development committee can identify and evaluate potential prospects for major gifts. By asking committee members to make notes on paper without speaking, the organization accomplishes two things at once. First, it protects confidentiality of prospect information. Second, it enhances the quality of the information about prospective donors through independent evaluation. Some suggested ground rules for silent prospecting are listed below:

1. The development committee (or prospect evaluation subcommittee) meets for prospect evaluation. Approximately 15 minutes are needed.

2. Staff provides lists of prospective new donors or current donors who might be asked to give at higher levels. Lists contain no previous gift amounts and no personal information. The purpose of the process is to test committee members' personal knowledge.

3. No one talks during the evaluation process.

4. Committee members record:

   • Gift capability, using scale such as A for the highest amount, for example: A=$100,000+, B=$50,000+, C=$25,000+, D=$10,000+, E=$1,000+, F=$100+ (members record only the appropriate letter).

   • The probability that the prospective donor might make a gift (using a scale such as 1 for the highest and 5 for the lowest) is also recorded.

5. Members sign their lists. No lists leave the room. All information recorded is left with staff and compiled in a composite report for each prospect.

6. Development staff follows up privately with members of the committee to learn more about identified prospective donors.

In soliciting gifts personally, the relationship between the board member soliciting the gift and the prospective donor is an important aspect of the process. Peer-to-peer relationship is most effective with a peer who has made a gift at one level, soliciting a peer for a gift on a smaller level. Figure 4 illustrates the criteria the development committee should consider in matching solicitors with prospective donors.

Conflicts of Loyalty

Because one of the legal obligations of a board member is duty of loyalty, board members should not use their relationship from one organization to solicit gifts for another organization. Individual board members may be comfortable in representing more than one organization to a potential donor who may have interest in both. The development committee should be aware of board members' commitments elsewhere and potential conflicts, and should coordinate assignments accordingly.

FIGURE 4
MATCHING ASKERS WITH PROSPECTS

Hierarchy of Effectiveness		
Advocate/asker relationship to prospective donor	Advocate/asker level of giving	Shared qualities
Peer/volunteer	Same as or greater than prospective donor	Economic status Social position Career status Mutual respect Interest in the organization
Proportionate giver/volunteer	Less than prospective donor	Mutual respect Interest in the organization Career status Social position
Staff/expert witness	Amount will vary greatly	Mutual respect Interest in the organization

Source: The Center on Philanthropy at Indiana University © The Fund Raising School.

A volunteer who has made a significant gift related to his or her means can be an effective solicitor for a larger gift if the relative significance of the gift is lower.

Preparation for Solicitation

Coaching is also helpful in preparing for solicitation of a gift. The idea of "training" can have a negative connotation, conjuring up ideas of boring and unproductive sessions that may not be effective or helpful. Board members, however, will usually accept coaching through one-on-one preparation, especially for major gift solicitation. Anyone involved in this process who has little experience will need opportunities for observing others, making joint calls, and essentially learning by starting slowly on tasks where they are likely to succeed. This type of training is also a good way to motivate board members' involvement in fundraising. As addressed earlier in the text, there is rarely a "one-size-fits-all" training or preparatory effort. Each board member holds his or her own strengths, weaknesses, and experiences, and it is up to the development committee to evaluate each board member, and think about how to involve him or her and who on staff or on the committee is best positioned to approach the person.

Many volunteers and/or members of the board will fail at fundraising without training and orientation: some members will fear rejection, others will see fundraising activities as imposing on personal relationships, and some simply will not know how to ask for the gift.

Development committee members should be trained to ask for gifts based on the case for support as discussed earlier in this book, rather than the power of personal relationships. This helps them avoid the fear of reciprocity. Development committee members must be able to articulate the case for support or the reason the organization exists, expressed in terms of values that the organization and the donor share. The case for support must provide a rationale for the programs that the organization provides to meet important public needs. This will assist in avoiding damaging relationships with friends and guarding against being solicited in return for projects in which they have no interest. The organization should provide training in making personal calls and asking for gifts based on their belief in the case for support. More experienced members should be asked to serve as mentors to new members.

The model in Figure 5 has been used successfully by The Fund Raising School to help train thousands of volunteers in gift solicitation.

FIGURE 5
SOLICITATION PLAN

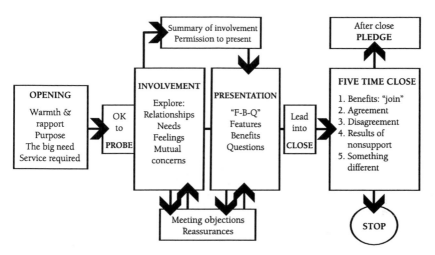

Source: The Center on Philanthropy at Indiana University © The Fund Raising School.

The Fund Raising School recommends a four-step solicitation plan as a structure for having a conversation about making a gift. The discreet steps of the plan are: the opening, the involvement, the presentation, and the five-time close.

The opening is an opportunity to establish warmth and rapport between the team representing the organization and the potential donors. Typically, solicitors will first make personal connections and/or connections to the organization. It is important to state the purpose of the meeting early on and to relate the purpose to the overall need in society being addressed by the organization. At every step in the process it is important to check for understanding and agreement and for permission to continue with the conversation. As the organizational representatives move from the opening to involvement phase, it is important for the donors to have a deeper interest in the cause.

The involvement phase requires listening. During this phase, the organizational representatives explore the relationships and feelings the donors may have with the cause that needs to be addressed. The organizational representatives should ask questions that will elicit information from the donors. Ideally , the involvement phase should end with a restatement of mutual concerns between the organization's solicitors and the potential donors. Based on mutual concerns, the organizational representatives can present a summary of the potential donors' involvement with the cause and ask for permission to present questions such as "Could we tell you about our plan to deal with this problem?"

Assuming the donors are interested in a presentation, the organization's representatives outline the features and benefits of the program and ask for any questions of the potential donors. It is typical at this point for objections to the program to be raised. In this instance the organizational representatives should address their concerns and, referring back to the program, outline ways to meet and deal with those objections. Should the objections relate to the cause, the organizational representatives need to move back to the involvement phase of the discussion. It is not always possible at this point to move directly toward the solicitation phase and a five-time close.

If the potential donors seem interested in the features and benefits of the program being outlined, it is time for the solicitors to move to the five-time close. Ideally, a member of the board or a volunteer will ask for the gift. The request should be for a specific amount, predetermined and based upon the prospects ability to give. Ideally, the solicitor will use such language as "Would you please consider joining those of us who are supporting this program by making a gift of $25,000?" Here, the solicitors should be silent. There are only three possible responses to this question. The potential donors can agree to the request, they can disagree and say no, or they can say maybe. If the donors say yes, details for the commitment can be negotiated. If the potential donors say no or maybe, it is important for the organizational representatives to explore the reasons why they are hesitant or unwilling. It may be the wrong time, it may be the wrong amount, or it may be that the solicitors have missed something in the involvement and presentation stages. At this point, the organization representatives can go back to the presentation stage and see if there are objections or questions. It is important to go through the request at least five times suggesting alternatives, addressing concerns, and ultimately discussing the impact of the donors not supporting the program. Finally, representatives can suggest something completely different, including visiting the organization, staying in touch, the possibility of talking about a gift at a later time, etc. It is important to stop and leave the relationship between the organizational representatives and the potential donors intact no matter what their response. Voluntary support should remain voluntary, and donors should never be made to feel guilty or isolated if they cannot support or do not want to support the project.

WORKING WITH RELUCTANT BOARD MEMBERS

Some board members may be reluctant to get involved in fundraising. Others may be experienced and enthusiastic. Fundraising is something that can be intimidating, despite experience level or passion for the organization's mission. The development committee can be helpful in facilitating the involvment of reluctant board members.

First, it is essential to provide board members with a thorough explanation of the rationale for fundraising and the role it plays in providing needed programs. It is also important to explain to new board members the reasons why the board itself needs to be involved in fundraising.

As we mentioned earlier, in many organizations fundraising occurs as the result of projected deficits in the budget. As a last resort, a board agrees (sometimes reluctantly) that fundraising might be necessary, at least in order to maintain current programs. The organization then sets out to raise funds in order to meet those immediate financial obligations. This default approach to fundraising can result in two incidences. First, it may leave the board less than enthusiastic about fundraising. Instead of focusing the board on raising funds for the fulfillment of the mission or vision of the organization, board members might be focused instead on a specific goal to meet immediate internal needs. Thus, potential donors will not be impressed by a board member who is focused on the urgent needs of the organization instead of the mission related to community needs. Second, donors are sophisticated enough to know when solicitors are asking because they are excited about the work of an organization and the potential the organization has, as opposed to asking under pressure because it is their duty and the organization desperately needs the funding.

In order to engage an unenthusiastic board, Lilya Wagner outlines three key ingredients for successful board involvement in fundraising in her article, "The Road Least Traveled: Board Roles in Fundraising":

1. Members need to understand the significance of their roles and how these contribute to productive nonprofits.

2. Board members and staff must acknowledge and deal with attitudes that hinder positive involvement.

3. Staff, with the cooperation and blessing of the chief executive and board chair, must communicate information — values, principles, practices — that leads to the adoption of appropriate board involvement."[3]

---

3. Wagner, Lilya. "The Road Least Traveled: Board Roles in Fundraising." From *Achieving Trustee Involvement in Fundraising.* Eds: Timothy L. Seiler and Kay Sprinkel Grace. New Directions for Philanthropic Fundraising, no. 24. San Francisco: Jossey-Bass, 1994.

Adapted from The Fund Raising School, there are five main steps that can be undertaken to work with reluctant board members:

1. Find one board member who is willing to be an example and work with him or her to encourage other board members to follow.

2. Bring in an outsider to train the board on the fundraising process including board members' roles.

3. Encourage hesitant board members to take part in less intimidating aspects of fundraising, including writing gift acknowledgments and appeal letters.

4. Develop board member job descriptions that include fundraising, and seek board members comfortable with fundraising and who have experience in that area.

5. Finally, it is important to take small steps in the evolution of a reluctant board into a fundraising board.[4]

As soon as a board member understands that fundraising is a natural, acceptable, and normal process in our society and within the nonprofit culture, it is easier for him or her to accept it. Feeling comfortable with the task radiates into the board member's manners and demeanor and helps turn the message into a likely and normal part of donor cultivation.

---

4. The Fund Raising School. *Principles and Techniques of Fund Raising*. Indianapolis, IN: The Fund Raising School, 2003.

6 ETHICS AND ACCOUNTABILITY

KEY ETHICAL ISSUES IN FUNDRAISING

Every board member has a responsibility to act ethically in serving the organization. There are unique ethical responsibilities related to the work of fundraising. Staff members must inform development committee and board members involved in fundraising about applicable ethical standards. Some key issues are discussed below that board members involved in fundraising should consider.

Obedience to the Law

Development committee members should understand all the legal aspects of soliciting a gift. This includes the value of a tax deduction for a gift if premiums or other benefits are involved. There may be state laws that regulate the solicitation of a gift even by volunteers. For example, in some states the organization's fundraising costs and audited financial statements must be disclosed at the point of solicitation. The development committee should also be familiar with state laws relating to solicitation and registration.

Confidentiality

Members of the development committee must maintain, in confidence, information about donors obtained through the prospect identification and evaluation processes. Information learned through one organization cannot be shared with another organization. Donors should be asked for permission if the organization wishes to share its donor lists with other organizations.

Respect for Donors

Members of the development committee understand the mission and goals of the organization and ask for gifts based on the case for support. Development committee and board members must not use relationships of power to obtain gifts. Members must respect the right of a prospect to decide freely whether or not to make a gift and at what level. Each board member should be familiar with the Donor Bill of Rights and ensure that organizational policies and practices adhere to its ethical standards. (Please see the Donor Bill of Rights in Appendix V.)

Prevent Self-Dealing and Conflicts of Interest

Section 501c3 of the Internal Revenue Code, which allows for deductibility of gifts to charitable organizations, specifies that no person associated with a nonprofit organization can benefit directly from the resources of the organization. Donors and board members should not expect preferential treatment for organizational business. Further, the board and staff members must avoid even the appearance of impropriety in all transactions. Therefore, it is essential to have an open bid process for all business and to be able to explain to the public any transactions with board members or donors.

Presenting Information to the Public

The development committee members need to be familiar with all fundraising materials the organization is sharing with the public and ensure their accuracy and properness. Committee members should regularly read the brochures they share with potential donors and visit the organization's Web site to make sure the image of the organization is clearly presented. The IRS Form 990 specifies fundraising expenses as a separate category. Financial statements should include fundraising costs. Board members must assure the public of the accuracy of financial information.

Assure That Funds Raised Are Being Used for Stated Purposes

The key to earning donors' trust is to show that their funds are used for the intended purpose. In the organization's financial books, according to generally accepted accounting principles, donations must be recorded as permanently restricted, temporarily restricted, and unrestricted net assets. Board members must be able to track expenditures so donors can see that funds for a particular purpose have been used that way. Also, development committee members and staff should regularly update donors on the evolution of the program or activity that they have funded. It is essential to keep donors posted on how their funds are used and the outcomes of their generosity.

Relying on Outside Consultants

If the organization hires outside fundraising consultants, the committee's role is to oversee that guidelines exist for appropriate compensation practices. Percentage-based compensation is not an acceptable method. A fixed-fee schedule helps ensure that the motivation of the consultant remains focused on long-term cultivation of prospects, not on immediate returns for maximum personal remuneration. As with staff, bonus incentives can be established only if they are based on performance, and not on percentage of funds raised. A competent consultant understands that fundraising is development of committed supporters for the organization, who remain loyal during the future campaigns as well. Cultivation of major donors is continuous. Results may not be evident for several years.

ACCOUNTABILITY OF OUTCOMES

Accountability and integrity are not necessarily the responsibility of the development committee, but they do have an impact on fundraising success. Committee members do not have explicit responsibilities in this case, but they need to be certain that accountability of outcomes and intensity of mission are being handled within the organization. Members of the development committee need to feel comfortable with promises they and others have made and they must continuously review outcomes *against* what is being promised. They must feel comfortable with the policies that protect the organization when its name is being used by a sponsor. For example, a health clinic would lose integrity if it allowed its name to be used by a tobacco company.

Holding the organization accountable includes developing indicators of success such as "dashboard indicators" in order to measure organizational performance in terms of outputs, outcomes, and impacts. This means presenting information to the public in terms it can understand. Fundraising maintains accountability when the process follows goals set by the board and when the board reports how dollars raised are supporting various programs. Fundraising activity brings the public into an oversight relationship as constituents are invited to examine the organization to ensure their contributed dollars are being put to good use for their intended purpose. All of these measures help keep an organization and its leadership accountable. Fundraising success is based on this level of accountability.

The chair of the development committee is ultimately responsible for making sure that the board focuses on fundraising outcomes. He or she is in the best position to coordinate the oversight of the fundraising plan and to review the reports from the various subcommittees.

One of the challenges in fundraising is that there is often more to do than can be accomplished with the human and financial resources available. Establishing priorities and key success factors can help a committee get a sense of where to begin and how to implement its goals. The following list provides critical success factors for fundraising in an organization:

- Strong support from the board, including individual giving

- Existence of a comprehensive fundraising plan

- Solid policies guiding ethical decisions

- Clear understanding of what the organization needs to accomplish its mission

- Reasonable and challenging fundraising goals

- Meeting of expectations to raise a certain amount

- Continuous communication with funders and donors

- Growth in donor base

Through dialogue between staff and members of the development committee, the ethical issues that the development team will confront in its work remain in the open and serve as a foundation for ethical behavior.

Conclusion

"Delegating work works, provided the one delegating works too."

— Robert Half

We end by returning to the beginning: Fundraising starts with the board. The development committee helps with the planning and implementation of the fundraising program by working closely with the development staff and by involving the entire board and often other volunteers as the process moves forward.

Members of this committee will have a special relationship to staff and donors — one that requires special attention to trust, accountability, and stewardship. The work of the committee is rewarding as funds are raised to meet important needs. Committee members must take the extra time and energy to prepare for action and have the ability to insert themselves in the community. Development committees may be proud to identify themselves as a goal-oriented group. Members of the committee must be adaptable and continuously ready to search for higher levels of achievement as the organization's needs change.

As promised, we have indeed explored the notion that finding success in fundraising secures your organization's future — providing a large slice to the whole pie of "good governance." Creating a special group that helps motivate peers and increases their comfort level while participating in the fundraising process may be the best approach you can offer to fulfill your organization's mission.

Appendix I

Charge to the [Board] Development Committee

Option 1

The role of the development committee is to ensure that the organization's total development program is in concert with the organization's strategic direction and needs. The committee serves as the mechanism by which board members and other volunteers are involved in the fundraising process.

The development committee is charged with focusing the organization and its board on fundraising. This includes constant attention to the strength of the mission and case for support, the organization's accountability, the involvement of constituencies with the institution, the resources required to carry out the mission, plans for soliciting the needed private funds, fundraising involvement, and demonstration of good stewardship.

Option 2

The development committee ensures that the organization has appropriate policies and guidelines for accepting gifts and donor solicitation. Its role is to encourage individual board members to participate in fundraising activities. It works closely with the development staff to build board members' capacities and to identify suitable involvement opportunities. All members of the development committee should also be members of the larger organizational development committee. (This option is more viable in an organization with strong development staff and/or an organizational development committee. The function of this particular board development committee is not as *operational* as option 1 in terms of fundraising.)

Charge to the Organizational Development Committee

The organizational development committee serves as the tool for the development staff to implement the fundraising plan. The committee gets actively involved in the various fundraising programs that the staff has outlined and organized. The organizational development committee consists of key board members, other volunteers, donors, and development staff. Key program staff also can help plan and implement the total development program. Responsibilities will include direct involvement in fundraising.

Appendix II

Job Description for the Development Committee Chair

The chair of the development committee provides leadership for involving the development committee and the rest of the board in the organization's fundraising process. The committee chair reports directly to the chair of the full board and works closely with the chief development officer CDO. The committee chair serves as a member of the organization's leadership development team along with the chair of the board, the organization's chief executive, and the CDO.

The chair of the development committee carries out the following duties and responsibilities:

- In concert with the CDO, schedules and prepares agendas for regular meetings of the development committee; develops potential subcommittees to carry out the work of the development committee; and establishes reporting structures for ensuring that tasks are carried out.

- On behalf of the development committee, reports progress towards meeting the fundraising goals to the board.

- On behalf of the organization, reviews and evaluates the performance of the development committee.

- Serves as a key volunteer in soliciting major gifts.

- Makes a gift to the organization that will be understood to be significant in terms of the personal resources the chairperson has available.

The chair should have a history of involvement with the organization that generates respect from other members of the board. He or she should have the organizational skills to assist the CDO in involving volunteers in the fundraising process, and the leadership stature to motivate other volunteers.

Appendix III

	Committee Members				
	A	B	C	D	E
Age					
Ethnicity					
Fundraising Experience					
Marketing Experience					
Writing					
Financial Management					
Database Expertise					
Legal and Planned Giving Skills					
Public Speaking Skills					
Leadership Potential					
Key Constituency					
Gift Level					
Other					

Appendix IV

SAMPLE OUTLINE: FUNDRAISING COMMUNICATIONS TOOLKIT FOR BOARD MEMBERS

Introduction

The purpose of a fundraising communications toolkit for board members is to provide them with the "tools" they need to effectively raise funds for your organization. As board members are often in a face-to-face situation where they are speaking with potential donors on behalf of the organization, this recommended toolkit focuses on providing key information about the organization to board members, often in a script format or a concise document with easily digestible bullet points. Information of this kind needs to be provided in *spoken* language, not written language, so that it is easy for board members to use the information in conversation.

Although the development of the toolkit will likely be a staff-driven project, the toolkit will be much more effective if it is developed in collaboration with the board members on the development committee. The development committee can make recommendations for the table of contents, review the content that the development staff prepares, and advocate the use of the toolkit to other board members.

This toolkit should be designed to be an easy-to-use reference tool. A clear and detailed table of contents or index is essential. There should be clear headers within each section, and plenty of white space on each page. Board members may sit down and read the toolkit all at one time, but they may just as likely refer to it only when looking for a particular piece of information. Therefore, some information may be included more than once in the toolkit (for example, a "key selling point" may also show up as a talking point about the need that the organization serves).

Finally, you may want to design and develop your toolkit so that it can be easily customized for particular board members. For example, you may have one board member who is interested in raising funds for a particular program. It would be helpful to have a fact sheet about that program in that particular board member's toolkit, but it would not be necessary to have the program fact sheet in every person's toolkit. You can decide which pieces from the "core" kit to include, and then have optional sections that can be added for particular board members as needed.

Highly Recommended Sections To Include

Talking Points about the Organization (e.g., The Case for Support Written for Conversation)

This section should include talking points about the organization, which will come directly from the case for support. A written case for support is often composed in language that does not feel natural when spoken and can often be quite lengthy. This toolkit should provide board members with a script that they can use to speak concisely and clearly with someone about your organization. Even though the essence of the talking points will come from the case support, it should not be the case for support verbatim.

Possible sections within this area include are listed below:

1. The "elevator" speech: How to describe your organization in two minutes.

2. Why should someone give to your organization? What is the need that you are addressing?

3. What does your organization do? Provide overview of programs and services.

4. Who does your organization work with? Who are its customers and clients?

Key Points of the Organization's Case for Support

This section will include impressive facts about your organization that catch people's attention. Some aspects of the key selling points may have already been included in the talking points section above.

This section could consist of particular authority your organization has ("We provide the seal of approval for 'X.'"); impressive information about who or how many clients you serve ("We serve over 1,000,000 people annually."); any impressive awards your organization has received ("We received the 'X' award from the state."); impressive statistics about how your organization is run ("We only have five paid staff but over 500 volunteers who make all of our services possible."); or the uniqueness/indispensability of the service you provide ("We are the only shelter for battered women in the five-county region," or "We are the only museum in the country solely devoted to children's literature.").

Outcomes, Evaluation, and Effectiveness

More and more, funders are asking nonprofit leaders the following question: "How do you know that you have been successful?" Board members must be able to answer this question confidently. Items that could be included in this section include the following:

1. Outcomes achieved by your organization, preferably in quantifiably measurable terms and as they relate to goals

2. Information about the evaluation efforts undertaken by your organization, and the results

3. Data about demand for your services

4. Data about efficiencies in your organization's operations

Stories and Testimonials

Recounting a personal story from a client is often the best and easiest way for a board member to talk about what your organization does. Also, board members often find testimonials personally motivating, which builds their confidence when fundraising. This section should include three or so of the best or most inspiring stories that are easy for a board member to relate. Be sure that no stories encroach upon a confidentiality agreement that the client may have with your organization.

How Your Organization Is Financed

More and more potential donors want to know how your organization is financed. This section should include information about the sources of income for your organization, such as earned income sources, government grants, foundation or corporate grants, and individual donations. It is also helpful to include some numerical data, such as

- earned income versus donations as a percentage of budget

- administrative/overhead costs as a percentage of budget

- fundraising costs as a percentage of budget

- unrelated business income as a percentage of budget

Other Possible Sections To Include in the Toolkit

Your organization may find it useful to include other sections in order to guide your committee members in solicitation and communication. The following list provides further possibilities, always leaving an open door for whatever works best for you:

- Fact sheets on primary programs and services
- Sponsorship opportunities
- Synopsis of a current strategic plan
- List of all funders
- History of the organization

Appendix V

Donor Bill of Rights

Philanthropy is based on voluntary action for the common good. It is a tradition of giving and sharing that is primary to the quality of life. To assure that philanthropy merits the respect and trust of the general public, and that donors and prospective donors can have full confidence in the not-for-profit organizations and causes they are asked to support, we declare that all donors have these rights:

1. To be informed of the organization's mission, of the way the organization intends to use donated resources, and of its capacity to use donations effectively for their intended purposes.

2. To be informed of the identity of those serving on the organization's governing board, and to expect the board to exercise prudent judgment in its stewardship responsibilities.

3. To have access to the organization's most recent financial statements.

4. To be assured their gifts will be used for the purposes for which they were given.

5. To receive appropriate acknowledgment and recognition.

6. To be assured that information about their donations is handled with respect and with confidentiality to the extent provided by law.

7. To expect that all relationships with individuals representing organizations of interest to the donor will be professional in nature.

8. To be informed whether those seeking donations are volunteers, employees of the organization or hired solicitors.

9. To have the opportunity for their names to be deleted from mailing lists that an organization may intend to share.

10. To feel free to ask questions when making a donation and to receive prompt, truthful and forthright answers.

The text of this statement in its entirety was developed by the American Association of Fund-Raising Counsel AAFRC, Association for Healthcare Philanthropy AHP, Council for Advancement and Support of Education CASE, and the Association of Fundraising Professionals AFP. This material was reprinted from www.aafrc.org.

SUGGESTED RESOURCES

Axelrod, Nancy R. *Advisory Councils.* Washington, DC: BoardSource, 2004. This book expands the traditional way of looking at the concept of advisory councils, exploring ways in which they can help the board to keep its own magnitude in check without losing impact. Nancy Axelrod proves that these groups have more functions than usually assigned, and explains the role an advisory council can play in helping your board to expand outreach efforts, find new supporters, incorporate new perspectives, and distribute tasks.

Bobowick, Marla J., Sandra R. Hughes and Berit M. Lakey. *Transforming Board Structure: Strategies for Committees and Task Forces.* Washington, DC: BoardSource, 2001. This book provides a fresh look at committees and how your board can use work groups to streamline the work of the full board. Discover the importance of reducing the number of standing committees and relying more on ad hoc groups and task forces.

George, Worth. *Fearless Fundraising for Nonprofit Boards.* Washington, DC: BoardSource, 2003. Author Worth George has developed a system that will help disinclined board members get started on their fundraising responsibility. By providing specific choices and instructions, this book helps to encourage once-reluctant board members to become active fundraisers. The book's centerpiece is a worksheet of 40 specific fundraising activities that range from simple to sophisticated, and all play an important part in the overall plan. With so many options to choose from, board members of every level of skill and experience can find a way to contribute to this critical role of fundraising.

Greenfield, James M. *Fundraising Responsibilities of Nonprofit Boards.* Washington, DC: BoardSource, 2003. Discover why fundraising is important and why board members should be involved. Included are practical suggestions for board members in direction, planning, and oversight of fundraising. Help your board succeed in the three phases of fundraising — cultivation, solicitation, and stewardship.

Howe, Fisher. *The Board Member's Guide to Fund Raising.* San Francisco, CA: Jossey-Bass Publishers, 1991. Written specifically for board members, the book is an accessible overview of — and rationale for — fundraising. It deals with the most likely questions and objections board members will encounter while fundraising.

INDEPENDENT SECTOR. *Obedience to the Unenforceable: Ethics and the Nation's Voluntary and Philanthropic Community.* Washington, DC: INDEPENDENT SECTOR, 2002. This publication provides useful information for staff and volunteers to understand the ethical dimensions of their own work. It distinguishes among illegal and unethical behavior and ethical dilemmas.

Lakey, Berit M., Sandra R. Hughes and Outi Flynn. *Governance Committee*. Washington, DC: BoardSource, 2004. Governance committees are essential in every board because of their ability to ensure full board effectiveness. This book illustrates how a governance committee not only recruits new members, but also transforms those recruits into productive and capable board members. The authors outline duties of the governance committee and provide helpful hints and guidelines on who should serve on this committee, how to determine what kinds of members your board needs, where to find these individuals, and how to orient and continuously educate your board.

Light, Mark. *Executive Committee*. Washington, DC: BoardSource, 2004. Executive committees are known to take on too much power, often resulting in confusion among the rest of the board members. Find out in which situations executive committees may be beneficial, and in what circumstances they may be a hindrance. Also included in this book is a description of who should serve on this committee and the intent of the committee's relationship with the board.

McLaughlin, Thomas. *Financial Committees*. Washington, DC: BoardSource, 2004. Accountability is increasingly important to nonprofits, and every board must be engaged in understanding its fiduciary duties. Learn about the core responsibilities finance, audit, and investment committees can hold. Placed with the important task of fiscal oversight and safeguarding an organization's assets, it is imperative that finance committee members comprehend the scope of their responsibilities. Discover how these committees can address challenges in helping the rest of the board understand complicated fiscal issues. This book will also help finance committees to stress the importance of board member independence in oversight and audit functions, and prepare the board to address potential new legal regulations.

Seiler, T.L. and Eugene R. Tempel. "Trustees and Staff: Building Effective Fundraising Teams." *New Directions for Philanthropic Fund Raising*. No. 4: Achieving Trustee Involvement in Fund Raising, 1994. This article discusses the relationship between trustees and staff members in fundraising. The entire publication is dedicated to various issues related to trustee involvement in fundraising.

Tempel, Eugene ed.. *Hank Rosso's Achieving Excellence in Fund Raising, Second Edition*. San Francisco, CA: Jossey-Bass Publishers, 2003. This book promotes an overview of the total development program based on the Rosso philosophy of fundraising. It includes chapters dedicated to trustee involvement in fundraising, team building, volunteer leadership, and ethics related to fundraising.

The Fund Raising School. *Principles and Techniques of Fund Raising,* 2003 edition. Indianapolis, IN: The Center on Philanthropy at Indiana University, 2003. The study guide outlines the process of ethical fundraising based on volunteer involvement. It includes a chapter on involving the board in fundraising.

About the Author

Eugene R. Tempel became executive director of the Center on Philanthropy at Indiana University on August 1, 1997. He has been closely involved with the Center since its inception in 1987, first helping to develop the concept for the Center and later chairing its organizing and policy committees. He serves on the Center's board of governors, and was the first elected president of the Nonprofit Academic Centers Council, a national organization of university centers dedicated to teaching, research, and service related to philanthropy and the nonprofit sector.

Dr. Tempel is a nationally recognized expert in the study and practice of philanthropy and nonprofit management. Since 1988 he has held numerous leadership positions in the Association of Fundraising Professionals, currently serving on its Ethics Committee. The *NonProfit Times* has named him in its list of the country's 50 most influential leaders in the nonprofit sector each year since the list was created.

A professor of philanthropic studies, higher education, and public administration, Dr. Tempel's career as a nonprofit professional also includes more than two decades of administration, fundraising, and teaching in higher education. He previously served as vice chancellor of Indiana University–Purdue University Indianapolis IUPUI and as vice president of the Indiana University Foundation. He is a member of several nonprofit and for-profit boards of directors, and is the immediate past chair and current member of the Indiana Commission on Community Service and Volunteerism.

Dr. Tempel is the author and co-author of several works in the field. He is the editor of the recently released book *Hank Rosso's Achieving Excellence in Fund Raising*, 2nd edition Jossey-Bass, 2003, and co-authored the book *Fund Raisers: Their Careers, Stories, Concerns and Accomplishments* Jossey-Bass, 1996 with Mar garet A. Duronio.

Dr. Tempel earned a Bachelor of Arts degree in English and Philosophy from St. Benedict College, a Master's degree in English, and a doctoral degree in higher education administration from Indiana University, and holds the Certified Fund Raising Executive professional designation.

About the Center

The Center on Philanthropy at Indiana University is a leading academic center dedicated to increasing the understanding of philanthropy — what it is, what motivates it, what impact it has — and improving its practice in the United States and internationally. The Center provides information, resources, and assistance to volunteers, board members, donors, nonprofit organizations, and public policy makers through a wide array of research, teaching, professional development and training, public service, and public affairs programs.

Founded in 1987 and headquartered in the Indiana University School of Liberal Arts at Indiana University-Purdue University Indianapolis, the Center seeks to build a closer relationship between research about philanthropy and nonprofit organizations and professional practice. The Center on Philanthropy is home to The Fund Raising School, which has taught more than 32,000 fundraisers on six continents the principles of successful, ethical philanthropic fundraising.

More information about the Center on Philanthropy and its programs, services, and resources is available on the Center's Web site at www.philanthropy.iupui.edu or by calling the Center at 317-684-8901.